# Just Grieve
A Companion in Times of Loss

Poetry by Lara Cullen

# For Evan

Copyright © 2021 Lara Cullen
Lara Cullen Studio

All rights reserved. No part of this book may be reproduced

in any manner whatsoever without written permission.

For information address:

Lara Cullen Studio

1151 Aquidneck Ave.

Middletown, RI 02842

www.laracullenstudio.com

ISBN: 978-1-7347273-2-6

*Just Grieve*

is a moment to pause;
to be with you
during your sadness;
sitting at your side;
heart wide open.

# Family

A single word,
encircling like a bird.
Love shared;
unwavering care.
Forever evolving,
never dissolving.
Devotion unbroken;
endless words spoken.
An invisible bond,
all this life long.
Roots like a tree;
the blessed family.

# A Love Poem

We will always be together
No matter how far we are apart
Your soul is right beside mine
Your heart is in my heart
I feel your every rhythm
Right down to my core
With a love as deep as mine for you
I could never long for more
Whatever force brought us together
Call it God, or chance, or fate
Is a blessing that can't be taken away
A bond that will never abate
My love for you runs so deeply
I can feel it pumping through my veins
When you came into my life
Nothing remained the same
As the tides rise and fall
And the world goes spinning round
Know I am forever beside you
Always feel me all around
We were given to each other
A love so tried and true
Everything that means anything
Leads me squarely back to you

# Empty

Emptiness
so vast and far,
swallowing me whole.
The current pushes,
but I am just
a blot
along for the ride.
If and when
this feeling will
cease,
is irrelevant now.
Blinded by
gloom,
and uneasy with
the prevailing
feeling of pointlessness;
now is not
the time to
develop beyond
seeing only
blank space
baring itself
before me.

# Goodbye to Yesterday

Today is not like yesterday;
yesterday was good.
But then I blinked,
and in a wink,
that life no longer stood.

I can't describe the feeling
when the world comes crashing down.
All I know
is time stood still,
while it crumbled all around.

The indescribable agony;
the guilt;
the emptiness.
No silver lining upon the clouds.
A future does not exist.

All I see before me now
through my tunnel vision sight;
is not a single reason to carry on,
when nothing will ever again
feel right.

Leave me now with my new today
as I say goodbye to last.
Let me fall into the darkness
until the storm has passed.

# Rain Fall Down

Let the rain fall down
it suits my mood,
sad and mellow;
grey and blue.
A dark cloud above
my soul reflects,
sun poking through;
its light deflects.
Moving by
the moments passed,
in time,
its strength will never last.
Refreshed and peaceful
the earth will find,
as the rain falls down,
in short time.

# My Love Lost

Should not the whole world stop
as mine has ended in a blink?
The future falls like dominoes;
impossible to face
the depth of loss that has taken place.
The heartbreak feels like the ocean;
drowning and powerful.
To face tomorrow without my love;
I will never make peace with the unfairness.
A life half empty,
a heart half full.
Replaying each second in my mind.
Stripped of everything;
this life will never hold the same luster.
Gone to Heaven;
a piece of me gone too.
Eternally bound together in spirit.
Until we meet again, my love,
I carry you in the void forever.

# Broken

When you realize
it can't be fixed
with glue, will, or hope.
That it is
broken;
beyond repair.
A slow exhale
as you place it
delicately in the trash;
as not to disrespect
what it was,
but to recognize that
it is no more.

# Take It Away

If I could take your pain away
I'd bottle it,
and toss it out to sea.
I'd watch it sail far away
from right now;
you and me.

I would wrap my arms around you,
and let you fall apart.
Let you cry until you're empty,
and we healed
your broken heart.

When I close my eyes
and picture you,
alone with your own tears;
I feel frustration knowing
that the cure will
take some years.

And right now is
for grieving;
together and privately.
I can't take your pain from you;
it's where you need to be.

# Grief

It comes out of nowhere,
and knocks you to the ground.
As a life you have always known
is left behind.
Like tunnel vision;
you see it in hindsight now,
wondering if it was even real.
Wondering how you will ever carry on
with this suffocating knot in your chest,
and grip on your throat.
How deep the pain is
as a spirit rips away from you.

They fly free.

With you left behind in pieces
scattered everywhere;
with no understanding of why
this had to happen.

Time will pass,
and life will keep going.
With a void in your heart forever.
Weighed down with memories,
regret, and a longing
for what could have been.
As deep and cutting as a
blade to the skin;
you want out now too.

You feel misunderstood,
watching life from a
bird's-eye view;
with darkness all around.

A transformation has taken place,
and although it was not for the better,
it is the new path.
The past life severed;
you must go on.

Grief-stricken;
a trauma victim.
You deserve every tear you shed
and let them fall
freely and without judgment
upon yourself.
Your strength
may surprise you,
but always stay true
to the rhythm within.

Grief will always be there,
like an empty shadow
following you around each day.
But then the shadow
becomes the new life,
and you have
become a new you;
and together, you rally up the strength
to put one foot in front of the other
to carry on;
at peace in this new skin.

# Ring Around the Moon

There is a ring around the moon tonight
glowing high above.
Invoking a certain eeriness,
and engulfing me in love.


I see faces in the moon at night,
and moments come and gone;
memories come flooding back
like the lyrics to a song.


The sky stands calm and still tonight;
stars dangle and gently glow.
If something is looming in my future,
I don't want to know.


The ring around the moon at night,
its wonder illuminates the unknown.
Completely lost in nature,
is where the spirit roams.

# Far Away Pain

Somewhere right now,
there is a pain
so deep
screaming out
from the bowels.
An agony
chosen at random.
Somewhere right now,
a heart is breaking in two.
Life changed forever
in a blink.
A hurt vibrating
and blinding.
As tears are released,
deafening cries
pierce the air.
Somewhere right now,
someone's whole world
has stopped.
A moment
in slow motion
as our world
keeps spinning around.
Somewhere right now,
it is someone
else's turn.
Blessed
are those
that it is not.

# The Shadow Man

He blankets me
at times unknown.
Darkness falls;
a call home.
A restless will
with no escape.
On this bed,
a new day waits.
Out of the corner
of my eye, he creeps.
A gentle soul;
he does not sleep.
A beam, a dash,
a blink, he's gone.
His voice is
what I truly long.
Whisper quietly;
I can hear.
But only through
a longing tear.
He delivers peace;
his message understood.
No one is ever
gone for good.

# Imitate the Wind

Imitate the wind;
invisible yet powerful;
quiet yet soothing.
Adapt as the wind does,
blowing around obstacles
in its path.
Know when to retreat
and be still.
Do not dictate
with strength and fury,
but maintain a breeze
and casualness.
Save the vigor
for when necessary,
and preserve the
the calmness,
and constancy
most days
will afford.

# Broken Heart

How do I live with a broken heart?
How do I find peace?
How do I find a reason to live
when the pain will never cease?
How do I find the point of tomorrow
when I long for yesterday?
The time before I lost my love
already seems so far away.
How do I accept only memories
where my loved one's soul once stood?
I thought I knew this life;
I thought I understood.
But now I feel I know nothing;
I don't know how to carry on.
This life will never feel right again;
everything is wrong.

An impossible void left to fill;
my Angel in the sky.
I want to lay right down beside my love,
and to all else, say goodbye.
How do I heal this broken heart?
Will I ever find joy again?
Or will I always look back on when
my love was here,
and know that was the end?
As I navigate these stormy waters,
with my newly broken heart,
please God, give me strength
to take each step;
and on me, your wisdom impart.
To know in time we will be reunited;
when it is my call to come home too,
but in the meantime, I will feel this break,
knowing there is nothing I can do.

# Why Children?

Why are children chosen
with so many others left to live?

What could God want in Heaven
that such innocence can give?

How is life so unfair
to those who deserve it least?

How do parents continue on
when their future has been ceased?

What is the point of any of it,
when you can have your
heart ripped from your chest?

One minute the world is one way,
you blink, and nothing's left.

How do you accept being robbed
of a life hardly lived?

How can you look to God,
and find a way to forgive?

The only reason to be given,
if there is even one at all;
is that it is better to have
loved and lost,
than to have never loved at all.

# Anchor Holding Nothing

Standing rusted
and almost forgotten
on the ocean floor,
a frayed rope
moves with the current
flowing all around it,
but the anchor
stays just as it is;
no longer holding
the vessel in its place.

It deteriorates
slowly through time,
with each new spec of salt
upon its metal surface;
eating away at what was once
vital to the ships
survival at sea.
The ship,
which has long moved
away from the unknown
of the ocean floor.

It will
float around;
travel thousands of miles;
see, feel and smell new things.
Yet it will never have the luxury
to stand idle in the sea again.

The anchor waits
because it has no choice.
It is heavy and stubborn,
never pushed or moved
by any storm around it;
stuck.
Buried deep in the sand
with years of damage,
it will remain this way
forever.

A sad
truth for the ship;
it must always sail on.
The anchor will forever remain
at the bottom of the ocean,
and the vessel always moving
away from it.

The anchor stuck in the same place,
but the ship stuck everywhere.

No matter how far it may travel,
or amazing sights it will see;
the ship will never know
the comfort of being still;
connected with the ocean floor,
and its anchor securely,
ever again.

# A Call to God

God,
are you there?
Do you hear my prayers?
Please do show me a sign;
my faith is wavering.

# Hero

With a bow of my head
And a heavy heart
I say with deep sorrow
Goodbye while we part

A loved one to many
A hero to all
Your courage was endless
And God gave you a call

A call to come home
And leave us behind
A void in our hearts
You live in our minds

Where the memories stay
As the pain dulls with time
But for now we all gather
To leave you behind

And we want you to know
As we say our goodbyes
With courage you lived
And with honor you died

# Dark Cloud

What
is this
dark cloud
hanging over
my head,
and will
the rain
ever cease?

# Hope

I close my eyes
and cross my heart,
wanting
all of life's wisdom
to impart;
a feeling of hopefulness
to get me through;
when there is nothing left
to say or do.

Fill my soul,
I'll blindly follow,
away from all the
pain and sorrow.
Deliver me back
to my life again;
no longer broken,
but on the mend.

# Death In Words

I can still see you so vividly.
It is as though you are right before me.
I keep waiting for you to round the corner,
and then a crushing feeling enters my body.
I have to stop and brace myself for impact.

You are gone now.

Where did you go?
I can no longer feel your energy in the room;
in this life.
My mind does not seem to be working right.
Did that really happen?

Everything from this point forward feels like
life before you, and life after you.
When I look out into the future,
it is impossible to think about it without you.

Never have I felt more present in my life,
and yet, so far away;
like I'm watching it all from overhead
looking down.
A witness, but not engaged;
from a vantage point of being on the
outside looking in.

But then it feels like it is only you and me.

Time will put distance
between the crush
of the first days without you;
time will forgive
some of the wounds sustained.

But life will never be the same again.

Someday when I look back
it is going to be hard to imagine a time
when you were here.

How spoiled I was then.

I never appreciated you enough.
I never told you how much
I loved you enough.
I never touched you enough,
and held you in my arms.
I feel consumed by regret,
and loneliness.
I can remember what it felt like
when you were still here.

It doesn't seem real.

The book slammed closed
and I was thrust forward.
Not into a new chapter,
but a new volume of this story of mine;
the part where I no longer have you.

# Blink

Do not take
for granted
the mundane day
because in the
blink of an eye
it can all be
taken away.

# Let Me

Let me be sad if I need to be,
let the tears stream down my cheeks.
Let the storm clouds come rolling in,
let me not crack a smile for weeks.
Let the world stop turning for a moment,
for a month, or a year.
Let everyone fall silent,
let my cries be all you hear.
Let me be a pessimist
and not see the brighter side of things.
Let me not care about myself
or what the future brings.
Let this moment come and go,
so that I can properly heal.
Let my sadness penetrate you,
and you can get a fragment of what I feel.
Let me reach out when I need to,
and push you away when I don't.
Let me want to kill myself,
I promise you I won't.
Let my sadness be my own to deal with;
let me hold it close and tight.
Let it be uncomfortable to see me this way;
learn for it to feel alright.
Let this time have no limit;
let it stretch on as it is needed.
Let the tears take time to subside
until my sadness has retreated.

# Stillness

Silence;
let me fill you
with my tears,
to heal in time
through many years,
and return again,
to what once
was me,
but for now,
in stillness
where I need
to be.

# Shadow of My Former Self

Emerging from the other side
I am but a shadow of my former self.
My energies depleted;
I have nothing left to give.

This new me is unrecognizable;
chewed up and spit out by life.
I am fragile.
Do not handle me as I once could be;
I cannot endure anything more.

So far from who I was.
I now mourn the loss of the life I knew before;
the one where I was strong and clear;
the one where I was sure.
I have been humbled by fear;
humbled by pain;
humbled by the unknown.

This shadow of my former self,
this new me I am forced to embrace;
will hopefully enlighten me,
bring new depth to my life;
attained as rites of pain.

I do not need to like it;
only accept it,
and hope that over time,
the shadow will become me once more;
finding my way into the light.

# New Step

Each new step we take

is a step into a new life;

onto a new path.

Each foot forward is a blind leap of faith

for what each day holds;

always remembering the fragility

of each moment we are granted.

# Found In Darkness

Look yourself
deeply in the eye
down to your core
until it is uncomfortable,
and you want to
look away.
Keep that blackness
in focus and keep going
deeper and deeper
until you don't know what
you are looking at any more,
and it is strange to see your own features.
You don't recognize
the reflection before you.
Flesh and bones
cannot hide the unknown
staring you back in the face.
A feeling of wonder;
of unlimited thought;
like getting lost in a maze.
You may want to avert your eyes,
but don't.
What you find in that blackness
may be a simple reflection.
Or maybe it is everything
you will ever need;
because what you are
looking at
is you.

# Nature Sings

The sky
is like an opera;
it sings its heart for you.
Mother Nature knows
you're gone,
and now is mourning too.
But instead of rain
the clouds cry out;
they dance across the sky.
God dipped his paintbrush
in your spirit,
and celebrates on high.
Earth speaks
the language of the soul.
I see you all around.
Everywhere in nature's beauty,
your presence
can be found.

# Peace

Surrounded by loved ones
You drew your last breath
Completely at peace
You were laid to rest

With no regrets
For the time we shared
You knew how much you were loved
How much everyone cared

Go now in peace
To Heaven above
We will miss you forever
But you live on through our love

# Relief

Turn the page
and look to see
a brand new day
staring back at me.

The storm has passed,
the road has veered.
Into a new life,
the clouds have cleared.

Light now shines
at the tunnel's end;
a mind, body, and soul,
blessed to mend.

During those dark days
it was impossible to see,
any reason for hope;
any sense of relief.

All faith was gone,
no bigger plan in sight.
It was a fight to march on;
nothing felt right.

Now, as those memories fade
and life moves ahead,
there is no longer anxiety,
desperation and dread.

Relief,
an almost indescribable feeling;
to take a deep breath
and no longer be reeling.

Lightness in each new step
being taken,
the past not forgotten,
no lessons mistaken.

Lessons of love,
heartache and fear;
will always stay close,
and perfectly clear.

But for now, I press on,
knowing this time could be brief;
when again, all feels right,
and I am filled with relief.

# Dust Cleared

The dust has settled,
and there is a silence so empty
it is haunting.
Everyone has gone home,
and resumed their lives.
With a look around
surveying the wreckage
there is no sense of relief,
but only a void;
where energy once was
and is no more.


A dazed walk
onto a new path.
A brain cloudy
and weighed down;
not working properly.
This life will never be the same,
and it will only ever take
a gentle gust of wind to send
particles flying everywhere
all over again;
consuming any strength gained,
and muffling the sounds of tears
for what was,
but is now gone forever.

# ARISE

And in time,
arise from your sorrow,
and into tomorrow,
a new day awaits;
a new life at stake.
Forcing your will,
to be of this world still.
Now quick, close your eyes,
and gather to ARISE!!

# Life Is Just a Layover

Life is just a layover
from where we come from and where we go,
and what happens when we die
is one of life's greatest unknowns.


I believe as our spirits float away
from their home of skin and bones,
that love totally engulfs us,
and we are not alone.


Loved ones are there to greet us;
God and Angels too.
Not with hugs and kisses,
and the things we humans do.


But with an energy that is infinite
and expands beyond the moon.
Everything makes sense,
and our consciousness becomes attuned.

We are filled with an understanding
unattainable to achieve while alive;
total peace falls over us,
and there is nothing left to strive.


There are so many things in this life
we want to do, and see, and learn,
but I believe as we leave this world
there is not a single thing we yearn.


And it is those who are left behind
that truly struggle when we die,
but our spirits soar high and free
becoming part of the sun-filled sky.


And the things that we have named
while we stood upon this earth,
don't mean a thing at all
in this moment of rebirth.

# New Day
a haiku

Awaken to a new day
Everything has changed
Life will never be the same

www.ingramcontent.com/pod-product-compliance
Lightning Source LLC
Chambersburg PA
CBHW061346040426
42444CB00011B/3120